How do you know the Easter Bunny is really smart?

Because he's an egghead.

Where does the Easter Bunny get his eggs?

From his eggplants.

Egg-cellent Easter Jokes For Kids

Frank Jackson

What happened to the Easter Bunny when he misbehaved at school?

He was egg-spelled!

Did you hear about the lady whose house was infested with Easter eggs?

She had to call an eggs-terminator!

Why do we paint Easter eggs?

Because it's easier than trying to wallpaper them!

What day does an Easter egg hate the most?

Fry-days.

What kind of bunny can't hop?

A chocolate one!

Why did the Easter egg hide?

He was a little chicken!

What do you call a rabbit with fleas?

Bugs Bunny!

Why was the little girl sad after the race?

Because an egg beater!

Knock, knock!
Who's there?
Alma.
Alma who?

Alma Easter
candy is gone.
Can I have some
more?

What do you get if you pour boiling water down a rabbit hole?

A hot cross bunny!

How do bunnies stay healthy?

Egg-ercise

Why won't Easter eggs go out at night?

They don't want to get beat up.

Why couldn't the Easter egg family stay for the picnic?

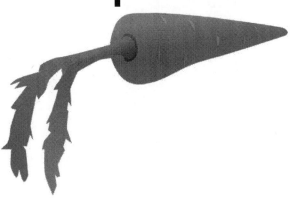

Because they had to scramble.

What do you call a mischievous egg?

A practical yolker!

What do you get when you cross a rabbits foot with poison ivy?

A rash of good luck.

What do you call a bunny with a book in his pocket?

EASTER

A smarty pants.

What do you call Easter when you are hopping mad?

Hoppy Easter!

How should you send a letter to the Easter Bunny?

By hare mail!

How is the Easter Bunny like Lebron James?

They're both famous for stuffing baskets!

Where does the Easter bunny eat breakfast?

At Ihop.

How long do spring ducks like to party?

Around the cluck!

What happened
to the egg when
he was tickled
too much?

He cracked up.

What do you call ten rabbits marching backwards?

A receding hare line.

What do you call a sleepy Easter egg?

Egg-zosted!

Why was the Easter Bunny so upset?

He was having a bad hare day!

How did the soggy Easter Bunny dry himself?

With a hare dryer!

Which came first, the chocolate rabbit or the chocolate egg?

Hmmmmmm?

What do you get when you find a rabbit with no hair?

A hairless hare!

Why are people always tired in April?

Because they just finished a March.

Knock, knock!
Who's there?
Arthur.
Arthur who?

Arthur any more
eggs to
decorate?

What happened when the Easter Bunny caught his head in the fan?

Happy Easter

It took ears off his life!

Why did the rabbit cross the road?

Because it was the chicken's day off.

What does the Easter Bunny get for making a basket?

Two points, just like anyone else.

How can you find the Easter bunny?

Eggs marks the spot.

Why was the rabbit rubbing his head?

Because he had a egg-ache!

Why did the Easter Bunny hop down the road?

He didn't know how to drive.

What's pink, has five toes, and is carried by the Easter Bunny?

His lucky people's foot!

What do you call the Easter Bunny after a hard day's work?

Tired.

Knock, knock!
Who's there?
Duwana
Duwana who?

Duwana
decorate some
eggs?

What's the Easter Bunny's favorite Story?

A Cotton Tale.

Why was the Easter Bunny arrested?

He was charged with hare-rassment!

What did the rabbit say to the carrot?

It's been nice gnawing you!

What did the bunny put over his sore?

A band-egg.

What has big ears, brings Easter treats, and goes "Hippity-BOOM, Hippity-BOOM, Hippity-BOOM"?

The Easter Elephant.

What do ducks have for lunch?

Soup and quackers!

What has long ears, four legs, and is worn on your head?

An Easter bunnet!

Knock, knock!
Who's there?
Heidi.
Heidi who?

Heidi the eggs
around the
house a little
faster, will ya?

Why is the Easter Bunny self-centered?

Because he is egg-ocentric.

Where does Valentine's Day comes after Easter?

In the dictionary.

Knock, knock!
Who's there?
Harvey.
Harvey who?

Harvey good
Easter everyone!

Made in the USA
Middletown, DE
30 March 2020